Violet's Violin

Written by Rachel Keyser

Illustrated by Donna Harley

Onion River Press

Burlington, Vermont

Text Copyright © 2024 by Rachel Keyser

Art Copyright © 2024 by Donna Harley

All rights reserved. No part of this publication may be reproduced, distributed, or transmitted in any form or by any means, including photocopying, recording, or other electronic or mechanical methods, without the prior written permission of the publisher, except in the case of brief quotations embodied in critical reviews and certain other noncommercial uses permitted by copyright law.

Onion River Press
Burlington, VT 05401
info@onionriverpress.com
www.onionriverpress.com

Paperback ISBN: 978-1-957184-81-4

Hardcover ISBN: 978-1-957184-82-1

Library of Congress Control Number: 202492194

*To all of my music teachers who inspired joy.
And for my daughter; my greatest gift.*

Violet excitedly glanced at the clock.

Today was her favorite day at school because she had music class.

But when music class was about to begin, Principal Hudson burst through the door. His voice boomed out loud,

"MUSIC CLASS HAS BEEN CANCELLED!"

Violet was heartbroken.

After school, Violet had many questions for her grandmother.

Why was her music class cancelled?

Where would she play her violin?

Who would she play with?

What could she practice?

As her grandmother led her up the attic stairs, Violet barely took a breath.

"Violet," said Grandmother calmly, "you may play here. But perhaps it is time you go find others to play with. Music is everywhere. There are many kinds of music, just as there are many kinds of people and places."

Grandmother kneeled on the attic floor beside an old trunk. She opened it.

"Here," she said to Violet. "This should be yours now. It was mine since I was a girl not much older than you. Share your music and follow the magic, wherever it may take you."

"I can't just play music anywhere!" said Violet, her eyes wide.

Grandmother smiled. "Music is a universal language, my dear. Do not worry. You will see. It's magical."

Violet did feel worried—and nervous, too—but she was also excited to share her music with others outside her music class. She held the violin close to her—the smooth maple wood of the instrument was warm in her hands. She raised the violin and tucked it under her chin.

Violet began to play. ♫♫♫

Violet was in France. Music filled the air around her with the sounds of street musicians.

Standing in front of a café, Violet watched three people perform. This was called a "trio." She noticed they were not using sheet music, and they played for people who were passing by. After a few songs, a new musician joined in for a tune. Everyone smiled, and there was dancing.

Violet wanted to join them.

"Bonjour," she said. "Do you know how to play "French Folk Song"? she asked shyly.

"Of course!" said the beaming bass player. "Won't you join us?"

Violet tapped her foot and followed the trio's lead. She had never played music you could dance to, and she had never played with a guitarist or a very big bass—it looked like a very, very large violin, and it was taller than she was! She started to feel at ease and watched as people in the café clapped. She grinned.

As the piece finished, the man who invited her called out, "I hope we can play together again, Violet!"

"Until we meet again!" She replied.

Violet began to play.

Now Violet was in South Africa. "Habari!!" she shouted over the booming sounds of the djembe drums that surrounded her. "May I join your circle?"

"Of course!" the children cried out, and they began to play louder and faster. Violet felt they were telling a story with the different volumes of sound. She sat down and listened to the rhythm of the drums, but she wasn't sure how to join in.

"Start on any note and play whatever you want," said a girl next to her. "We call that improvising!"

A woman held her rumba shakers high in the air, and Violet began to play a simple tune on her violin. She didn't know where that tune had come from, but Violet kept playing, and the music poured out of her easily.

"Wow!" said Violet when they finished. "That wasn't any music that I know!"

The drum circle clapped and the girl said, "It was your song!"

Violet liked this a lot, but it was time to discover a new place. She waved and replied, "Until we meet again!"

Violet was enjoying exploring the world. Her grandmother was right. Music really was everywhere!

Violet began to play.

Violet was in Greece. She couldn't believe she had already played music on her violin along with so many different instruments. She had even created her own song.

"Yassou!" Violet waved to the small group sitting on the rocks. A boy was strumming a familiar tune on a long-necked instrument.

"I know that piece," said Violet, and she began to play along with him.

"I learned it on the violin!" said the boy when they had finished. "Now I play it on the bouzouki. Would you like to try?"

The strings were similar, and Violet plucked out the tune slowly. She had never tried a different instrument before, but she enjoyed using her ears to figure out the piece. Violet loved it so much! Could she find a bouzouki at home?

"Thank you for letting me play!" Violet handed the instrument back to the boy.

"I hope we meet again," said the boy.

"Until we meet again," said Violet.

With music everywhere, Violet was feeling more confident. She thought about her music class. She had already played with so many new people. Though she enjoyed playing violin by herself, making music with others made her feel joyful. She wasn't ready to stop.

Violet began to play.

Now Violet was in Switzerland.

"Grüezi!" Violet greeted the musicians who were gathered.

An older man gestured his violin in the air with such joy at the sight of seeing her! "A musician!" he shouted. "Come and join us!"

Violet beamed. They played music for hours, until the sun set and the moon began to shine.

"Do you play together every day?" she asked.

"No." The man shook his head. "We play together once a week. Sometimes there are two of us, and sometimes there are ten of us. And sometimes people sing and yodel! It doesn't matter how many of us there are, we're just happy to share our music as much as we can."

What an excellent way to spend your time, thought Violet. "Thank you so much," she said. "Until we meet again!"

Violet had one more place she wanted to go.

Violet began to play.

Violet was in Japan.

"Konnichiwa," she said. She noticed musicians setting up for rehearsal. "What are you going to play?" she asked.

"We are rehearsing our Japanese folk song, "Sakura," a woman with bright eyes explained. "Sakura means 'cherry blossoms,' and we are celebrating the signs of spring."

"May I join you?" asked Violet.

"Of course you can!" The woman smiled and showed her the music. "Today, my violin group wants to rehearse under the cherry blossoms."

Violet loved the melody they played. It was simple and sweet. She enjoyed playing outside in the shade, and she really loved playing a traditional Japanese folk song.

Soon enough, Violet felt it was time to return home and tell her grandmother about all the places she'd played music.

"Thank you." Violet waved to the group. "Until we meet again!"

When she got home, Violet made her way back down the attic stairs with new questions on her mind.

Would she be able to find enough musicians to start her own group? Maybe she could start a band. Maybe she would find a guitarist or a flutist to play with, and they could all play under a giant tree!

The possibilities seemed endless.

Time passed, and Violet kept playing her violin every day. She practiced old music and new music.

She practiced playing by ear. She practiced music she had learned from around the world. She even wrote a song for her grandmother that she named "Evelyn's Reel."

She missed the friends she had met all over the world on that magical day. But what she missed most was sharing her music with others!

She was no longer nervous to play music with others or to try new things on her violin.

Summer came and went. A new school year was about to begin. There was no news from Mr. Hudson about her music class, and Violet began to wonder what to do.

If she could share music, maybe others might join her!

Soon an idea started to blossom, and suddenly Violet knew exactly what she wanted to do.

You are cordially invited to Violet's Benefit Concert

*Friday, August 26th, 6:00 p.m.
Morris Auditorium*

This concert is to help Morris Elementary's Music Class. This concert is dedicated to all musicians near and far. This concert is for anybody who loves music. Please join me in sharing my music with you.

*Warmly,
Violet*

VIOLET'S PLAYLIST

Danish String Quartet: Shine You No More
Yo Yo Ma: Sakura, Sakura
Dreamer's Circus: City Gardens
Bach: Concerto for two violins in D minor
Northern Resonance: No. 1
Nickel Creek: Cuckoo's Nest
Mark and Maggie O'Connor: Appalachia Waltz
The Gothard Sisters: Hummingbird
Beethoven: Symphony No.5 in C minor Op.67
Bouzouki Kings: Ah Helidoni Mou
Massenet: Meditation from Thais

Rachel Keyser grew up as a Suzuki violinist in Vermont. This is her first children's book, which is vastly inspired by aspects of her own life. When she is not teaching violin in Vermont full time, you can find her outside, practicing, playing music, skiing, and most importantly, traveling with her family. Rachel enjoys anything musical, especially when it comes to working and being around kids. She's had a violin in her hand for over 30 years and looks forward to sharing this book and her music. She can be found online at RachelKeyser.com

Donna Harley is a painter and illustrator, living in South Burlington, VT. She appreciates the gifts, and magic, that music can bring to everyone... everywhere.

Printed in the USA
CPSIA information can be obtained
at www.ICGtesting.com
JSHW040816111124
73193JS00006B/12